The Contemporary Condition book series offers a sustained inquiry into the contemporary condition from a range of perspectives by key commentators who investigate contemporaneity as a defining condition of our historical present. Contemporaneity refers to the temporal complexity that follows from the coming together in the same cultural space of heterogeneous clusters generated along different historical trajectories, across different scales, and in different localities. With the overall aim of questioning the formation of subjectivity in time and the concept of temporality in the world now, it is a basic assumption that art can operate as an advanced laboratory for investigating processes of meaning-making and for understanding wider developments within culture and society. The series identifies three broad lines of inquiry for investigation: the issue of temporality, the role of contemporary media and computational technologies, and how artistic practice makes epistemic claims.

Sternberg Press

THE CONTEMPORARY CONDITION

THE CONTEMPORARY CONDITION 16

I Can't Sleep
Lionel Ruffel

Translated by Claire Finch

Published by Sternberg Press, 2021

Series edited by Geoff Cox & Jacob Lund

Published in partnership with ARoS Aarhus Art Museum and The Contemporary Condition research project at Aarhus University, made possible by a grant from the Danish Council for Independent Research, September 2015–August 2021.

The translation has been funded by the research unit "Fabrique du littéraire" at University of Paris 8.

ARoS
AARHUS ART MUSEUM DENMARK

AARHUS UNIVERSITY

DET FRIE FORSKNINGSRÅD
DANISH COUNCIL FOR
INDEPENDENT RESEARCH

contemporaneity.au.dk

Design: Dexter Sinister
Printing and binding: BUD Potsdam
Paper: Pop'Set Cloud

ISBN 978-3-95679-603-6

Sternberg Press
71–75 Shelton Street
London WC2H 9JQ
www.sternberg-press.com

Distributed by The MIT Press, Art Data, and Les presses du réel

Can’t Sleep

Lionel Ruffel

Translated by Claire Finch

LETTER TO JACOB LUND

"My dear friend,

I'm sending you a little book that, without injustice, could be said to have neither head nor tail, since everything, on the contrary, is both head and tail, alternately and reciprocally."

You may recognize, my dear Jacob, the letter that Charles Baudelaire wrote to his publisher on December 20, 1861, to present his *Petits poèmes en prose.* Modestly (we are talking about prince Baudelaire, after all), and if you will allow me to do so, I would like to make his words my own in order to present you with my own "little book." I'm doing this modestly, even if counterintuitively, as you are well aware that the Baudelaire letter is one of the most definitive manifestos for a specifically *modern* way of writing.

I don't know if these words come to mind because I am reading and commenting on the Baudelaire letter in the pages that follow, or if I am reading and commenting on the Baudelaire letter in the pages that follow because I had the impression from the start that I was writing a book that was not quite in tune with the invitation that you and Geoff originally extended to me. Knowing you, my dear friend, *docteur ès anachronismes*, I'm sure you prefer the second hypothesis.

This misalignment is surely another part of our shared history. You launched your series, The Contemporary Condition, the same year my book *Brouhaha, les mondes du contemporain* was published. The timing was off, even if we were almost in sync. Within a few months, we made up for it. In the end, we met happily, in full agreement and camaraderie, and decided on a contribution that I would make to your series. And then what happened? And then nothing, until today, and the transmission of this "tortuous fantasy," to ventriloquize Baudelaire again.

This little book may surprise you, especially since it doesn't match the various books I've promised you over the past three years. I hope to convince you that as tortuous as it is, this fantasy, and perhaps for these two reasons, because it is tortuous, and because it is a fantasy, I hope to convince you that this tortuous fantasy responds better than all my other texts to the objective of your series: to offer "a sustained inquiry into the contemporary condition."

Although it all depends, and I'm sure you agree with me, on the forms and conditions of the inquiry.

Without being aware of it, I somehow set a trap for myself in *Brouhaha*, by calling for a contemporary writing of the contemporary. Not to be outdone, I tried to answer my own call, following a few basic tricks and principles.

First of all, a principle of inversion that may seem childish to you but which, in addition to being amusing and emancipating, is, I find, terribly effective.

If thinking, according to modernity, means thinking from above and from afar, I began to think myopically, with my nose in the matter and my hands in the sludge. If thinking in modern terms is to think at a distance from oneself, I began to think on the basis of my experiences, because any proposal concerning the world needs to be put to the test of self-analysis.

If, meanwhile, to write (theory) in modern terms is to have something to say, to plan it before starting, if it is to have a beginning, a middle, and an end, if it is to privilege monological and unidirectional objects, then I chose to move according to the uncertain, the unfinished, the erratic. If, finally, writing in modern terms means postulating objectivity, then I chose to flourish in subjectivity and its undoing.

Admit that it's fun standing on your head.

But it's not just fun. For the form of the investigation is not distinct from its purpose. It can even completely invalidate it.

I have a little confession to make, my dear Jacob. Of course, I remain in admiration of the great modern treatises on our contemporary condition, which subsume it into a few clear and unambiguous main ideas. I remain admiring, but I never quite believe in them, and in the end I grow tired of them. In any case, I am no longer able, assuming I have the means, to play that game.

I would like to take this opportunity to tell you, my dear friend, that I am neither dogmatic nor authoritarian; everyone does as they want and as they can. The path I have chosen since *Brouhaha* (notably in the book that followed: *Trompe-la-mort*) is, in my opinion, radically anti-authoritarian on this point. It is nourished by other anti-authoritarian and minor writings that have become my "beacons," to use a term dear to Baudelaire, or rather, the poles by which I orient myself in the contemporary. For this text, the four poles of my compass were Christine de Pizan (1364–1430), Michel de Montaigne (1533–1592), Victor Klemperer (1881–1960), and Nathalie Quintane (1964–). Only one of them is contemporary to us in the sense of sharing a temporal period. Yet they are all my contemporaries, in the sense of the temporal complexity that we argue for, because they help me to think—that is to say, write—this present that we conceive, you and I, as charged with and crossed by multiple temporalities.

This attitude towards writing is a way of answering (forgive the scholastic nature of the demonstration) the third line of inquiry that your series has determined for itself, "how artistic practice makes epistemic claims," if we consider that theoretical writing can be an artistic practice.

But I believe, dear Jacob, that my tortuous fantasy also responds to the first two: “the issue of temporality, the role of contemporary media and computational technologies.”

We so often talk about time and temporality when we investigate the contemporary, but more often than not it is by forgetting that we constantly and multiply experience it (Saint Augustine rolls over in his grave). I used the exceptional circumstances of this year (pandemic, lockdown) to work with time.

My tortuous fantasy was written during the daily hour that I managed to wrest from domestic and educational life, between the beginning and end of the first mandated lockdown in France, which lasted from March 13 to May 11, 2020. I hope, my dear Jacob, that you will feel, in reading it, the consistency of the passing time, and of the time it has taken since then to take it up again and rewrite it.

These circumstances, to say the least, break the historical continuum and form a “constellation saturated with tensions,” as the contemporary beacon Walter Benjamin has written. They reflect both the most immemorial and the future, the day before yesterday and the day after tomorrow, and not only “yesterday and tomorrow” (those magnets of modernity). But we always begin in the present.

For those who weren’t sick or dying, or in great social, psychic, and physical suffering, this constellation mainly saturated time by overloading it with media viruses, to use a metaphor that I’m not sure is still a metaphor. To a certain extent, with its effects of global synchronization, of capturing attention, of controlling populations, and then the generation of all the forces that resisted it, this pandemic is a caricature of our contemporary condition. In the course of our own lives, it was and remains at the time of this writing an extreme experience.

I don’t know about you, my dear friend, but from the delirious profusion of discourse that has accompanied this time, this logosphere gone mad, I have the impression that I haven't learned anything that I didn't already know. Of course, I haven't learned any more from the—based on what I've read—ridiculous lockdown diaries that have sprouted up and will soon invade the bookstores. And yet, I was thinking that it would be useful to put the best of this discourse to the test of experience.

I have another little confession to make. It was while flipping for the twentieth time at least through the books of Yves Citton, Jonathan Crary, Bernard Stiegler, and Paul B. Preciado, always with Walter Benjamin in mind, that I came up with the idea of writing a contemporary life. Not an abstract life, as was Baudelaire's ambition, but a very concrete life (at least I think so): my own. My own life reduced to two activities that were particularly strained at the time: reading and sleeping. Reading and sleeping in the heart of (and despite) the logosphere and the media streams.

The text could have been called "The Contemporary Condition of Sleeping and Reading," but frankly, "I Can't Sleep" sounds better, plus it's true.

Don't ask me, my dear friend, if this is a fiction or a theoretical text. I don't know, I no longer recognize these distinctions. It is certainly an essay, in Montaigne's original terms, and as we still understand it in French: an attempt to grasp our contemporary condition, as closely as possible.

It's an attempt in which the contemporary theorist in me becomes a seismograph, and not an interpreter.

Say hi to Geoff for me,
Devotedly yours,
L.R.

PS: You will see that following your request—and I thank you for it, because I had fun doing it—I added a lot of footnotes, which form a second text proposing a rather explicit theoretical frame of reference.

I CAN'T SLEEP

Stuck

Yesterday I was there again, I had about thirty pages left before I finished reading a big book[1] that I always said I had read even though it wasn't quite true, although I had read two thirds of it over the course of several sessions. We all do that, don't we? But this time, the whole world was stuck, I told myself that it was now or never. I had three or four hundred pages left, it was perfect, I had the time to get started and to let it last long enough, let it stabilize, or at least I had the evenings, after a succession of household and logistical tasks. Once started, I still had to find the solution to a problem. Reading big books is uncomfortable and difficult. And sleep is not kind to me, I need a thousand rituals to fall asleep, of which a certain bodily comfort is one. It's not that I don't like this book, in fact I really do like it, I mean I wouldn't say I love it, but I do like it very much. It's just that it makes my hands numb when I hold it for too long, it weighs on my plexus when I put it down. There is always a moment when my demon wakes up and forces me to leave it on the pile of books waiting for me: my personal hell,[2] or rather purgatory,

1. Roberto Bolaño, *The Savage Detectives* [1998], trans. Natasha Wimmer (New York: Farrar, Straus & Giroux, 2007).

2. Translator's note: "Hell," or *l'enfer* in French, refers to the restricted section of the French library in which works that are considered obscene are stocked. Researchers can access these works with special permissions.

books that I love very much but that don't match with my rituals.[3]

This book, however, has the consistency of my nocturn readings, the ones that prepare me for sleep. But since sleep is unkind to me, I absolutely need, and I mean absolute need, to read to fall asleep, even when exhausted, even after a night of insomnia, even when jetlagged, even after love, even when drunk, even when satiated, even when ill, even when under the influence, always, always, always. At least a few lines, a few pages. And when sleep eludes me in the dark, I open a book again and resume the ritual. It's bad enough as it is, but what's worse is that I can't read just anything. I can't be stupefied by just any prose (because it is always prose) that falls into my lap, so whenever I have to go somewhere, I have to carry a stack of books like others carry a stack of pharmacy boxes. I've done that too, but that was before, now I don't need a pharmacopoeia, instead I take a very large, thick cloth bag full of books. I can assure you, it's heavy. I've never been able to bring myself to cut down, to compile them all into a single object, an iPad, or an e-reader, a portable bookcase.[4]

3. At home, these stacks multiply. Especially the ones devoted to these daytime readings that are almost always fragmentary, chopped, and discontinuous, and thus always uninterrupted. The books are always there and ready for me, and I am potentially, but rather rarely, always ready for them. Sometimes I remove one and replace it when it has fulfilled its function, which was not necessarily to be read. They form the landscape of my interests and they sustain me. Right now, on two coffee tables set up in the living room, one finds (I'm only giving the date of their initial publication): Victor Klemperer, *Language of the Third Reich: LTI, Lingua Tertii Imperii* (1957); Tiphaine Samoyault, *Traduction et violence* (2020); Jérôme Baschet, *Adieux au capitalisme* (2016); Achille Mbembe, *Brutalism* (2020); Susan Sontag, *Illness as Metaphor and AIDS and Its Metaphors* (2001); Roland Barthes, *The Preparation of the Novel* (2010); and a bilingual edition of Shakespeare's tragedies (*Titus Andronicus, Romeo and Juliet, Julius Caesar, Hamlet, Othello*). That's the first table. On the second: Vinciane Desprets, *Au bonheur des morts, récits de ceux qui restent* (2015); Felix Denk and Sven von Thülen, *Der Klang der Familie: Berlin, Techno and the Fall of the Wall* (2014); Romain Huet, *Le vertige de l'émeute* (2019); Franz Kafka, *Diaries, 1910–1923* (2009); James C. Scott, *Against the Grain: A Deep History of the Earliest State* (2018); Nathalie Quintane, *Les années 10* (2014).

4. There is one history of portable libraries that I recommend. You will find it in Enrique Vila-Matas, *A Brief History of Portable Literature* [1985], trans. Anne McLean and Thomas Bunstead (New York: New Directions, 2015).

That's for daytime, when the screens invade us, but not for nighttime, not for sleep. No.

So before any departure, but also before choosing a book, one must project the consistency of the night readings by opening several volumes, testing them during the day, which is sometimes misleading. I have experience, but I still sometimes fail. The dosage is subtle, and moreover it changes slightly with time, with my time and that which surrounds and forms me. I generally know what I reserve for daytime readings: discontinuity and staccato, speed. I don't need excitement to fall asleep; we all know that one last line before going to sleep has never worked. But once you get rid of staccato and discontinuity, you're not much further along. So when I test, it's first a matter of words and wording. It has to be consistent, it has to be resistant, I have to be able to lean on it and keep my balance, not to go through it too quickly or abruptly, not to get caught, but not to be jolted, either. The wording must lead to reverie, and a gradual slide into sleep. I then mentally switch from the standing position to the lying position. There are so many beloved books that I can't read at night. Duras, for example: it's not possible, too staccato. Shakespeare: too much dialogue, too much discontinuity, too much strangeness. No essays of course, the limit is *Tristes Tropiques*, with its consistent sentences. It can't be too much fun either, like Quintane, I love Quintane but I can't fall asleep with it, or with Rabelais or Sterne, either, as I'm sure you can imagine. I can't do it, and it's even worse when the writing fades away to leave more room for storytelling,[5] when hypnosis tries to hide its tricks,

5. In France, efforts to theorize "storytelling" have given way to a high-flying debate between an apocalyptic Left (Christian Salmon, *Storytelling: Bewitching the Modern Mind* [2008], trans. David Macey [London: Verso, 2010]) and a Left of empowerment and hope (Yves Citton, *Mythocratie: Storytelling et imaginaire de gauche* [Paris: La Découverte, 2010]). Sorry to my international readers, but as a typical Good French Intellectual, the only debates that I care to weigh in on are those happening between different branches of what remains of the Left.

or when I'm in front of what feels like a televisual flow: that doesn't work either. And that's it.

Sometimes the consistency is perfect, it's almost miraculous. When I was younger, and I regret that it doesn't happen to me anymore, I used to read a lot of this one French author, super high-class style, Nobel Prize and all, long sentences, present participles in spades, hyper highbrow I don't even know if people still read him. At that time, not so long ago, he was quite a cult among the young reader that we were. A Nobel effect perhaps, which must have lasted twenty years, if the work of this one author is any example. After that, it goes out of date.[6] So I read him day and night. By day, I was frantically scribbling notes and remarks;[7] by night, I'd slip into his work so easily that I'd end up dreaming about it.[8] It's not a metaphor, those were my actual dreams.

I would dream the next part of it, I would fall asleep until the book fell out of my hands and woke me up and I could, just for a brief moment, compare the prose in the book with what my dream had made of it. It was really miraculous, I think it marked the beginning of something, a miracle or maybe a curse, I don't know, because from then on I understood that nothing distinguishes fiction from life; that nothing in our lives exists that is not filtered by

6. To understand literary temporality, one should read all of Pascale Casanova's works, in particular, "The Literary Greenwich Meridian: Some Thoughts on the Temporal Forms of Literary Belief," *Field Day Review*, no. 4 (2008); or *The World Republic of Letters* [1999], trans. Malcolm DeBevoise (Cambridge, MA: Harvard University Press, 2005). To understand literary spatiality, one should still read all of Pascale Casanova, for example, *Kafka, Angry Poet* [2011], trans. Chris Turner (Kolkata: Seagull Books, 2015). And finally, to remember that literary criticism, like other human and social sciences, is a combat sport, one must really, but really, read all of Pascale Casanova. To her, from whom I have learned so much, I dedicate this short text.

7. Especially in *Histoire* or *Les Géorgiques*, which I was writing a master's thesis on. Claude Simon: *Histoire* (Paris: Éditions de Minuit, 1967); and *Les Géorgiques* (Paris: Éditions de Minuit, 1981).

8. Especially his final books, *Le jardin des plantes* and *The Trolley*. Claude Simon: *Le jardin des plantes* (Paris: Éditions de Minuit, 1997); and *The Trolley* [2001], trans. Richard Howard (New York: New Press, 2004).

the fictions that surround and produce us. I also felt, without understanding it, and this is surely the most essential, that we communicate through dreams, and that this is what attached us not to the world, but to the multiplicity of worlds.[9] While everything else kept us away from it. I began to see insomnia as a form of illness for those who could no longer communicate with the multiplicity of worlds other than through fictional machines. You will have noticed, moreover, that a lot of films feature these fictional matrices, these sorts of vortexes, where dreams are connected. Generally it's quite frightening, we often see a hybrid between spongy masses and metals, between light signals and organic heat.[10] Can you see it? Who would really want to be trapped in that?

In any case, if my dream was chasing the book I was reading, then I'm sorry, and you can say what you want, but literature (fiction, dreams, magic, religion, whatever) is not separate from the world and life. That's it, I'm back, as usual: I'm already responding to the criticisms that I haven't been given yet but that I'm so often given and that I'm sure I'll be given again if I end up getting through this. I am always being told: You should be making better use out of what you have. You, who knows your classics, your moderns, your contemporaries, couldn't you use all of that to say something, for once, about the world, about politics, about the current crises, about how we're actually experiencing things or how we should be experiencing them. Instead of rehashing your old mystical, illuminated tales of dreams that communicate. As if we haven't had enough of your old stories. The world around us deserves that you dedicate yourself entirely to its

9. Philippe Descola, *La composition des mondes: Entretiens avec Pierre Charbonnier* (Paris: Flammarion, 2014).

10. Recent examples of excellent specimens: the third season of the series *Westworld* and the first season of *Devs*. The Wachowskis' *Matrix* trilogy (1999, 2003) has produced a dominant imaginary.

analysis. Don't you have anything better to do with your state-subsidized life?[11]

Yes, yes I know, I even think I tried at one time or another, but I can't do it, I'm sorry, I can't do it, I don't know how to do it; I tried and believe it or not, when I was dreaming of the sequel to the Nobel Prize books, I was also dreaming of being a philosopher, a philosopher who expresses himself in the public sphere, and who is admired for his ideas, a pop star of thought.[12] Except that the one who I idolized, the one who made me an intellectual worker, always shunned and despised both the spotlight and spontaneous reflection. Although there were still his books, fantastic, so inspiring. The ones written with his schizoanalyst coauthor,[13] those are what made me, I owe them almost everything, along with cold wave, rave parties, frater-sorority, and love. It's funny, I hadn't understood at the time that the power of those books was formal, not really textual, even if their speed, their inventiveness, were also on the scale of the word and the sentence. They had a power that was more than form, even; it was a power of echo, of repetition, of arrangement and resonance, and I didn't understand, until recently, that that is the only thing I have inherited from them (certainly not the power, but, more modestly, the manner), that this is the

11. Dear international reader, in case you come from the worldwide academic market, you might be interested to know that a university professor in France is paid by the state, and is theoretically a civil servant for life. Of course, there has been talk of putting an end to a system that is not very conducive to the liberalization of the academic market. As I write these lines, in the summer of 2020, while gatherings of more than ten people are forbidden and everyone is on vacation, the government is forcing the passage of a law for the "modernization" of higher education and research that is supposed to put an end to this French anomaly. Before the lockdown, the university community as a whole was marching in protest of this bill.

12. Of course, I didn't know it at the time, but I was dreaming of becoming a Judith Butler, Achille Mbembe, Paul B. Preciado, or Donna Haraway.

13. Deleuzo-Guattarianism, or maybe we should call it Guattaro-Deleuzianism, has been deployed in four essential books. Gilles Deleuze and Félix Guattari: *L'anti-Œdipe: Capitalisme et schizophrénie 1* (Paris: Éditions de Minuit, 1972); *Kafka, pour une littérature mineure* (Paris: Éditions de Minuit, 1975); *Mille plateaux: Capitalisme et schizophrénie 2* (Paris: Éditions de Minuit, 1980); *Qu'est-ce que la philosophie?* (Paris: Éditions de Minuit, 1991).

thing I can claim. In what we perceive, some things repeat themselves, while others are different.[14] Making this record, putting it to music, is finally what I have dedicated my life to so far.

Recently, as we were stuck together, and the talkative people had little choice but to multiply their hysterical speeches until it got to be deafening, on the networks reappeared, as sometimes happens, a bit of a video of the philosopher—of course, I've been talking about Gilles Deleuze. He was talking about art and resistance, talking about cinema and ideas, talking about control societies, talking about the difference between creation and communication, talking about information as a transmission of slogans,[15] it really was so powerful, deep, and illuminating about what was happening that it crushed all the other talk, all of the biggest and most futile chatter in the history of humankind.[16] But above all, the speech was carried by this voice, a voice that was already fragile and yet strong and supremely free, free especially of the notes that his eyes almost never refer to. Even speaking without notes he resists playing the star, giving a show. As a result, I watched the *Abécédaire* again.[17] This is so much what we intellectual workers should have taken as an example. Instead, it is almost the opposite that has happened: institutionalization, power, personal branding. You get it.

14. Giles Deleuze, *Différence et répétition* (Paris: Presses Universitaires de France, 1968).

15. Go here, it will make you feel better: https://www.youtube.com/watch?v=2OyuMJMrCRw&t=1826.

16. And this is coming from me, who has elsewhere taken a very positive view of what I named the contemporary "brouhaha," and the contemporary as brouhaha. Yet here I was dreaming of silence. Lionel Ruffel, *Brouhaha: Worlds of the Contemporary* [2016], trans. Raymond McKenzie (Minneapolis: University of Minnesota Press, 2018).

17. *L'abécédaire de Gilles Deleuze* is a film produced by Pierre-André Boutang, composed of interviews between Deleuze and his former student Claire Parnet. I discovered that you can access it without leaving your home, via a channel that even seems legal. Just follow this link: https://www.youtube.com/playlist?list=PLiR8NqajHNPbaX2rBoA2z6IPGpU0IPIS2.

So I told you, I tried and I can't do it. And if I can't do it, it's probably because I don't believe in it. Now, it's too bad, I'm too old, I'm not going to try anymore, I'm hopeless. I must be one of the last romantics, seeing echoes and correspondances,[18] it's the only explanation I can see. And I believe in it, so I'm holding on, I'm digging, even if I'm getting farther and farther away, I'm digging, I'm digging and I believe more and more. It's like the gold rush: a prospector gradually moves away from the group and finds himself completely isolated, and from Robinsonade to Robinsonade he eventually finds that he's not so badly off, he realizes that it wasn't gold he was looking for but something more elusive, which doesn't really have a name, like a wave that undulates, like "the clouds—the clouds that pass—yonder—the wonderful clouds."[19] So I dig and, even though it's my own grave that I'm digging, I believe in it more and more.

For example, with this story of day and night readings, and subsequently that of sleep, believe it or not, I have the impression that I have never thought about a subject that's as philosophical, as political, or as contemporary.[20] Because we all sleep, don't we? It doesn't matter whether you fall asleep at the snap of a finger or with fear in your stomach. Or whether you fall asleep overcome by anguish, or happy

18. Charles Baudelaire, "Correspondances," in *Les fleurs du mal* (Paris: Auguste Poulet-Malassis, 1857).

19. Charles Baudelaire, "L'étranger," in *Le spleen de Paris* (1869), accessed September 30, 2020, https://fr.wikisource.org/wiki/L'Étranger.

20. For the section that follows, and for many other things, I acknowledge my great debt to Bernard Stiegler. Especially for the development and deployment of the pharmakon concept that he takes up from Derrida who himself was reading Plato. The pharmakon is a remedy, a poison, and a scapegoat; every technique and therefore every medium is a pharmakon. It is difficult to refer to a single book in such an abundant bibliography whose books, moreover, are constantly revisiting, enriching and responding to one another. For those who have never read this work, a good introduction to the pharmakon can be found in Bernard Stiegler, *What Makes Life Worth Living: On Pharmacology* [2010], trans. Daniel Ross (Cambridge: Polity, 2013). In the summer of 2020, we learned of his passing. So I dedicate this text to him as well.

as a baby, or hypnotized by letters, images, or sounds. Of course, in the absolute it does matter, but not for what I am talking about now.

So let's start from here: we all fall asleep at one time or another. Sleep connects worlds, animal and plant species, it connects times and eras. It also distinguishes them, because we don't all fall asleep in the same way, and there are certainly one or several contemporary conditions of falling asleep. Depending on places and times, we fall asleep differently and sleep takes on different implications.[21] So find me anything that's more philosophical or more political, that's more essential, in a sense. Of course, there are reproduction and food, but I wouldn't know what to say about those, whereas sleep, for better or for worse, is my specialty. As a literary theorist and as an insomniac, the two being neither totally interchangeable, nor totally distinct.[22]

But I can see very well that a literary theorist who talks about sleep is not the sexiest thing in the world. If you're a cinephile that veers towards recent releases, then when you put sleep and reading in the same sentence, you start drifting, and you find yourself in a bedroom in Brooklyn. At the back of the room, there's a bed. Then on either side of that bed are the bodies of Adam Driver and Scarlett Johansson, both absorbed by the book they're holding in their hands, and even though they're both super sexy, frankly, it's not really a dream to read in bed if it's going to separate couples, pushing them to prefer the isolation of reading to the warmth

21. If only there were a Foucauldian history of sleep.

22. Pierre Pachet, *La force de dormir* (Paris: Gallimard, 1988). My apologies to you, international reader, for all of my obscure French references. If you find equivalents in any language or lingua franca, do not hesitate to send them to me at lionel.ruffel@univ-paris8.fr. Thank you. That way you can do as Geoff and Jacob did who, once they received my letter, directed me to Matthew Fuller's remarkable book, *How to Sleep: The Art, Biology and Culture of Unconsciousness* (London: Bloomsbury, 2018). Luckily they didn't make me read it before, I think if they had, I would never have written my tortuous fantasy. And if in the previous note I wrote that a Foucauldian history of sleep was missing, now that I've read Fuller's book, I don't think so. And—surprise, surprise—this contemporary investigation of sleep is neither a history nor Foucauldian. But it is exciting, you have to read it!

of embracing bodies.[23] And if you're more of a classic movie buff, you know that this will all be screened in Paris, with Antoine Doinel and Christine, who produced the original scene that was the cover image for the 1970 film *Bed and Board*.[24]

And it's true that in these scenes, that's all we see: the isolation of unembodied bodies that read, incapable of tasting the pleasures of the flesh, hellishly conventional, I mean, petty bourgeois. Think, instead, of all the hot scenes that take place in beds, with naked and muscular bodies panting, twirling, filled with intensity, enjoying without restraint. Think of all the crime scenes that take place in bedrooms, where drug dealers exchange their merchandise for money with big shots and suddenly, *pam! pam!* it goes wrong and it's a massacre. Think of all the scenes of espionage, voyeuristic or ultra-technological, think of the scenes in hotel rooms, which open up all kinds of fantasies, think of all those conspiracies that are born in bedrooms, against all that, frankly, Scarlett and Adam in their pajamas and their bourgeois comfort doesn't make you dream.

And yet these scenes exist, they are many, I would even say that there are more of these reading-in-bed scenes than there are of the scenes where we fall asleep in front of the TV, slumped in a sofa. I've always found the scenes of falling asleep in front of the TV very interesting, especially the choice of show that the character's watching. As an aside, if I had to do it all over again, I would devote my scholarly life to studying the movies shown in the movies, it must be super relaxing. So these scenes of couples reading in bed, if they exist to the extent that we could devote several doctoral theses to them, then they must tell us something. In the beginning we are distracted, we see objects, clothes, decoration, bodies that are nonathletic and constrained by reading, which arouses quite a bit of contempt. We also see

23. *Marriage Story*, a film by Noah Baumbach, 2019, streaming on Netflix.
24. François Truffaut, *Domicile conjugal*, a film from 1970.

what looks like a lack of communication, at least if we define communication as talking or hugging. While these scenes might be similar to those of reproduction or eating, it is in them and only them that we see testimonies of what might be the most essential to us: falling asleep, and doing so by relying on an artifact, here a book, but it could be something else, a screen for example, so that the fear stops and the reverie begins.[25]

A Night Hunt

But back to the point. I told you that when I was younger there was that miracle that made me dream about the books I used to read. Unfortunately, that miracle is no longer happening. It's like the first high, you always chase after it, but you know it's never coming back. Now I understand, I don't look for intensity so much,[26] on the contrary, I run away from it, I keep it for the daytime readings, the ones that keep me awake. The thickness of the wording, the consistency, that's what I am looking for, that's what reassures me. The subject, the period, the style itself doesn't matter, only this thickness, this consistency that resists me without stopping and that welcomes and envelops me. You have to get to know and meet what the prince of modern poets used to call, always a little ironically, well, you never know if it is ironic or not, but still, he talked about the "lyrical movements of the soul," the "undulations of reverie," the "sudden jolts of consciousness."[27] And I have the impression that reading at night, before going to sleep, this neurotic and modern ritual of

25. We could call these artifacts screens. Like their ancestors, the screens that stood in front of chimneys, they filter out the excessive heat that otherwise consumes us.

26. Tristan Garcia, *The Life Intense: A Modern Obsession*, trans. Abigail RayAlexander, Christopher RayAlexander, and Jon Cogburn (Edinburgh: Edinburgh University Press, 2018).

27. Charles Baudelaire, "Lettre à Arsène Houssaye" (December 20, 1861), accessed September 30, 2020, https://fr.wikisource.org/wiki/À_Arsène_Houssaye_(Baudelaire).

the Western petty bourgeois is one of those privileged fields that should not be neglected. And all the more so, since it connects us—especially those of us who like me, or I should say, in spite of myself, are just as neurotic, modern, petty bourgeois—to other rituals that are neither modern, nor neurotic, nor bourgeois, nor Western. Since these connecting devices are not so many, we shouldn't neglect this field; on the contrary, we should try to explore it.

So I'm exploring it. I realized that I could not, or could no longer, as my mind was occupied with the affairs of the world, make the end of a book coincide with falling asleep. If I have less than thirty pages left, I prefer to postpone reading it until the next day, and then I will do it during the day, which changes a lot. For a few years now, the end of books have been ruined, because often, during the day, I am in a hurry, I am caught up in social and work time, media time as well, not in this time, which is also social, of course, but nevertheless more attentive to the "lyrical movements of the soul," the "undulations of reverie," the "sudden jolts of consciousness" that sleep forms: a more primordial time, so to speak, that struggles against the first one, against the social time, work time, media time, without ever totally defeating it, at least in my case.

So that's what happened to me again. I was heading towards the end of this big novel that I said I'd been reading for several years when I realized that I might finish it before I fell asleep. It gets worse. Feeling the end coming, and doing more than feeling it, because an object like a book has the peculiarity that you literally see the end of it, the sudden jolt to consciousness took precedence over the undulations of reverie, relegated to the background, as if automatically put on hold, and the sudden jolts jolted forward, *hop hop!* are we there yet? is it soon? how much further? how many more pages? what's going to happen?[28] and a different kind of attention was put in place, a regime of alert,[29] which is fundamentally that of awakening.

But it is also that of danger or hunting, of predation. Of the proximity to a death that is coming, a violent death, one that doesn't leave you in peace. For the death that is announced, the nonviolent death, sometimes engenders the undulations of reverie.[30] I remember seeing an old animal die, and having tried, because I loved him deeply, to feel as close as possible to what he was experiencing, to share it. He no longer had those sudden jolts that so often disturbed him, he slept calmly. A veterinarian told me that he was nevertheless devoured by the disease, and probably overwhelmed by the pain. Sleep helped him to fight fear.

If I have to finish a book, I'm either hunter or prey, my stomach gurgles metaphorically, *crave*,[31] I'm hyper-conscious, I can't fall asleep. I run after sentences and sentences run after me, *crave*, I have a tendency of compelling the continuation without having read it, of sensing it without discovering it. And that's not possible, the reverie fades before consciousness. And then, there is something else: this excitement that doesn't offer any peace forces me to open another book, and then it is the excitement of a new

28. I was thinking that these jolts have something to do with the invasion of the present by the future, which happens through prediction and preemption. Some have named this invasion as the new and essential characteristic of the contemporary. See Armen Avanessian and Suhail Malik, eds., *The Time Complex: Post-contemporary* (Miami, FL: [NAME], 2016).

29. Dominique Boullier, "Les industries de l'attention: Fidélisation, alerte ou immersion," *Réseaux*, no. 154 (2009/2): 231–246.

30. And it does this for those who rest, as well as for those who pass. For more on this, see Vinciane Despret, *Au bonheur des morts: Récits de ceux qui restent* (Paris: La Découverte, 2015).

31. This word comes to me in English in the middle of what was written as a French text because of, or rather thanks to, the musician Léonie Pernet, who made it the title of one of her albums. I really like the mixes she produces from political and social news. See https://soundcloud.com/leonie-pernet.

beginning that seizes my nervous system.[32] It can work when you have planned it, when you've scheduled in the day to start a book at night, but you never know if the wording will work for your undulations, so it's risky, if you're in full jolt you have the double risk of the end, then the beginning. If we want to undulate, if we want to move lyrically in order to fall asleep, we must always read in the middle, never leave the middle of the fictional matrix. This is another lesson from the wonderful Scheherazade that I like to talk about so often.[33] Faced with her predator, this hungry tiger that only thinks of devouring his prey and getting it over with, she offers him the infinity of the narrative read aloud. There will be many endings, but the end never coincides with the dawn that the king's deranged mind has instituted as the moment of sleep, satiated by sex, revenge, and violence. She makes reading something other than a hunt, she hypnotizes, she undulates the reverie that soothes and puts you to sleep. About myself, about my own life, I learn every day from Scheherazade. And even if I don't put anyone at mortal risk, I sometimes wish she were there by my side, to curl me up in the middle of the hypnotic womb, where dreams communicate. Then I'd fall asleep.

A Dark Prince

But now I've talked about the prince, so his music keeps running through my head, and I couldn't find peace without playing it. It won't last all night, but like an old hit heard on the radio in the morning,[34] that's all I can hear now. It's not even off-topic, I can allow myself this discrepancy, because

32. On this subject, I really should take the time to reread Jean-Marie Schaeffer, *Why Fiction?* [1999], trans. Dorrit Cohn (Lincoln: Nebraska University Press, 2010).
33. Notably in Lionel Ruffel, *Trompe-la-mort* (Paris: Verdier, 2019).
34. Peter Szendy, *Hits: Philosophy in the Jukebox* [2008], trans. Will Bishop (New York: Fordham University Press, 2012).

when he evoked the sudden jolts, the movements, the undulations, he understood that the world, at least the world he knew and described, the modern and capitalist world, had finished with sleep, that it had become insomniac, in a state of permanent wakefulness, of hunting and predation. Of course, we're still sleeping, but as I've read elsewhere,[35] sleep has been overtaken and it's already lost. We no longer sleep what an earlier version of this dark prince imagined to be "the sleep of the beasts."[36] His *Flowers of Evil* made him famous, but he knows that this monument was the last of a bygone era, that the correspondences were for before, when we still, even if less and less, communicated through dreams. So he changes; not everything, but he changes radically to favor wakefulness over sleep.

He wrote a very brief text, which reads as luminous, dazzling even, now that we no longer know how to sleep. Whether it could be read as all that or not when we were entering the insomniac pandemic, I don't know. It is addressed to a man whom he calls "my dear friend," although it is hard to see what kind of friendship could unite the dark prince who has dedicated his life to the spending of life,[37] and the cultural entrepreneur who has dedicated his to the accumulation of wealth through the press, literature, theater, culture, and real estate projects, all of which are almost interchangeable.[38] But this "friend" runs *La Presse*, a major daily newspaper where the prince would like to place his new project, prose poems. So go for "friend," and even "dear friend," especially when talking to someone who weighs so much financially.

35. Jonathan Crary, *24/7: Late Capitalism and the Ends of Sleep* (London: Verso, 2013). Along with the works of Bernard Stiegler, it is this book by Jonathan Crary that has had the greatest influence on this text.

36. Gérard de Nerval, "Le Christ aux oliviers," in *Les chimères* (Paris: Michel Lévy Frères, 1856), 295–297.

37. Georges Bataille, *La notion de dépense* (Paris: Lignes, 2011).

38. This interchangeability is evident in another work by Jonathan Crary, *Suspensions of Perception: Attention, Spectacle, and Modern Culture* (Cambridge, MA: MIT Press, 2000).

He tells him that he is sending him a "little book," yes, you understood correctly, the demigod of the monumental *Flowers of Evil* is sending him a "little book." This is of course false modesty, because he knows full well that this "little book," or *petit ouvrage* in French, thus doubly but falsely devalued, for I don't know about you but I don't trust any words that end in -age, I tell myself that irony always permeates them, apart from the word "courage" perhaps, anyway he knows that it is in this "little book" that he produces his greatest poetic revolution, a revolution that marks the end of dreams and sleep. At best, after the revolution, after sleep, we'll have snapshots of reverie that respond to and bypass or even, we can dream it, resist this 24/7 wakefulness. And he will be, as always, the cursed prince, from now on almost glib. "There isn't much poetry at the moment," he might say, as one of his heirs will say one hundred and fifty years later.[39]

He uses a reptilian metaphor, mythical for people like me, presenting us with the little book that "could be said to have neither head nor tail, since everything," he continues, "on the contrary, is both head and tail, alternately and reciprocally." No more great works, long live the small works, those that offer "admirable convenience." I can imagine. How he must have suffered before finally resolving, in a masterful way, like the prince that he is, to use a word so far from the ideal: "convenience"! How he must have suffered, before amusing himself with it, to say that this convenience does not only concern him, but also a distinguished "you," the dear and industrious friend! How he must have suffered, before empathically embracing the project, seeing that this convenience also concerns the readers, who are no longer the cursed brothers of the

39. Noémi Lefebvre, *Poétique de l'emploi* (Paris: Verticales, 2018). Alert to all editors, translators, and readers of French works: this book is, in my opinion, one of the most exciting books written in French recently.

Flowers of Evil, always in search of an ideal, but a people of workers newly literate and "on vacation" like in "Le vieux saltimbanque," a people exhausted by the work of the week and the day, and who, from reading, can only hope for a temporal suspension of capitalist alienation: an alienation that now knows no limits, and is the seat of sleep and dreams. "On such days it seems to me the people forget all, sadness and work; they become children. For the little ones, it is a day of leave, the horror of the school put off for twenty-four hours. For the grown-ups, it is an armistice, concluded with the malevolent forces of life, a respite in the universal contention and struggle."[40] Yes, he must have suffered, but he has resolved to do so, it is in the interstices of the armistice that he now writes.

Of this suffering, there remains only irony, a lucidity streaked with cuts. "We can cut wherever we want," he said to his dear friend, "I can cut my reverie, you the manuscript, the reader his reading." The image of the snake begins to take shape, and from one casual moment to the next, a horrific image is revealed, a vertebra is removed, it is chopped into many fragments that gradually become sections. When you think about it, it's a bit disgusting as an image, and yet it is intended to "please" and "amuse" the dear, industrious friend for whom it is intended. But as you have heard, what is first "cut" is the reverie, which can only take shape in an object, a manuscript destined to be industrialized and chopped to pieces, for a fragmentary reading. Half a century ahead of its time, this is Taylorism applied to the movements of the soul. Does this make you want to sleep and dream again? From the outset, he evacuates the other possible response

40. Charles Baudelaire, "The Old Montebank," trans. Joseph T. Shipley, in *Baudelaire: His Prose and Poetry*, ed. T. R. Smith, accessed August 12, 2020, https://www.gutenberg.org/files/47032/47032-h/47032-h.htm#Page_66; and in the original French, "Le vieux saltimbanque," in *Petits poèmes en prose* (1869), accessed October 9, 2020, https://fr.wikisource.org/wiki/Le_Vieux_Saltimbanque.

to fragmentation, which consists in suspending "the reader's restive will from the endless thread of fine-spun plot," this seriality that since then and still today forms the dominant imaginary of industrial capitalism, the acceptance of the armistice. This is the solution that comes to occupy the available brain time[41] that alienation concedes so as not to kill its agents too quickly, while they are still productive. Many people are satisfied; we, too, find satisfaction in the armistice, as long as we do not see another solution.

And it's true that I also feel this admirable convenience when I tell myself that I'm too tired to watch a movie that lasts two hours, whereas I'm not too tired to watch two one-hour episodes of a series. Time has little to do with it, indeed nothing to do with it, because, beyond all philosophical considerations, two hours of a movie is just as long as two hours of a series. But the serial format offers this promise of armistice that the film format doesn't offer me, or at least doesn't offer me anymore, or perhaps never again will. It reminds me of the words of a certain great thinker born at the end of the nineteenth century, who died on September 26, 1940, in Portbou while fleeing the Nazi threat, he who will be for eternity the best interpreter of the dark prince, and a prince himself. Already in exile, in one of those short texts that seems to us to contain the meaning of an entire life and of all

41. In 2004, the CEO of Europe's largest private television channel, TF1, defined its core business as follows: "There are many ways of talking about television. But from a 'business' perspective, let's be realistic: at its core, TF1's job is to help Coca-Cola, for example, to sell its product [...]. But for an advertising message to be perceived, the viewer's brain has to be available. Our programs are designed to make it available: in other words, to entertain it, to relax it and prepare it between two messages. What we sell to Coca-Cola is available human brain time [...]. Nothing is more difficult to obtain than this availability. That's where the permanent change happens. You have to constantly look for programs that work, follow fashions, surf on trends, in a context where information is accelerating, multiplying and becoming commonplace." Quoted in Les associés d'EIM, *Les dirigeants français et le changement* (Paris: Éditions Huitième Jour, 2004).

life itself, "The Narrator" or "The Storyteller,"[42] according to the choice of the translator of the German "Der Erzähler," he compared narrative (the story) and the novel and said: "Actually, there is no story for which the question 'How does it continue?' would not be legitimate. The novelist, on the other hand, cannot hope to take the smallest step beyond the limit at which he writes 'Finis,' and in so doing invites the reader to a divinatory realization of the meaning of life."[43] Maybe that's why I can never finish a novel before going to sleep, maybe it's because I can't bring myself to feel the sudden jolts of this death that invites me to reflect on the meaning of life. "What draws the reader to a novel," he says, "is the hope of warming his shivering life with a death he reads about."[44] Of course, warmth is important, but feeling death can also chill. A tale never ends, it is always taken from a previous story and announces a future one, it plunges us into the matrix. In each storyteller "there is a Scheherazade who thinks of a fresh story whenever her tale comes to a stop."[45] There is some of this, of course, first in the newspaper feuilletons, and later in TV series. The serial seems to plunge us into a matrix of infinite dreaming where we are no longer ourselves, and where we hope to find rest. Whereas at the end of novels or films, death lurks, vertiginous.

42. Translator's note: In French, Benjamin's "Der Erzähler" has been translated as "Le conteur" or "Le raconteur," while in English it has been translated simply as "The Storyteller." The nuance we miss in the English is between the French *conte*, story, and *raconter*, to tell a story. *Conteur* thus puts the emphasis on the person telling the story, whereas *laconteur* shifts focus to the telling of that story.

43. Walter Benjamin, "The Storyteller: Observations on the Works of Nikolai Leskov" [1936], in *Selected Writings, Volume 3, 1935–1938*, ed. Howard Eiland and Michael W. Jennings, trans. Edmund Jephcott, Howard Eiland, et al. (Cambridge, MA: Belknap Press of Harvard University Press, 2002), 155.

44. Benjamin, 156.

45. Benjamin, 154.

I feel this quite frequently, when the evening comes, when the rigors of daily logistics have passed, when I no longer want to work, organize, care for, provide sustenance, when the night comes and I know that at some point or another I will have to face the sleep that so often escapes me that I will need all these rituals of fiction, these progressive immersions, first through the moving image, then through reading; according to the undulations of my reverie, it will be tale or novel, film or series, hoping that the two will merge, echoing the lyrical movements of the soul without the sudden jolts of consciousness. I sometimes feel that I don't have the courage to face the film's terminal form, the form that consumes and leads to death, and that series represent this admirable convenience of life always continued. I am also aware that before their advent, before their undivided triumph, my craving for moving-picture fiction was less demanding. That's how it is: the more that voracious capitalism expands its empire, the more insatiable our need for nocturnal fiction becomes. Sometimes I can start one in the middle, other times I prefer to watch two episodes of a series that I will never finish, and there I understand the danger that lies in wait, in this false reverie that is nothing more than a permanent awakening, an occupation, that multiplies ends and beginnings ad infinitum to keep us in forced wakefulness, eyes wide open to the infinity of consumption and unfulfilled need. That's why for my nocturnal readings, I prefer long narrations that take me away from the end, I transform them into ancient tales, I never finish them, because the contemporary tales offered to us in series are tales that have been metabolized by capitalism. They still have that ancient element that soothes the fear of death, but watching them is like taking amphetamines, in that they only delay our need to sleep and dream.

The prince understood all of this, long before anyone else, with his serial prose poems, mass-produced.

He understood that our dreams, our fictions, communicate with our economy.[46] He understood that the voracity of capitalism requires more and more fiction to keep its workers both awake and stunned. He understood that voracity occupies our days and nights, to make us forget death, but at the same time to make us forget life. So the demigod reacts, telling us, "It is especially the frequentation of huge cities, the crossing of their innumerable relationships, that gives birth to this obsessive ideal." It then becomes a question of describing "modern life, or rather a single and more abstract modern life." And finally, there is the formula that people like me know almost by heart: "Which of us has not, in his days of ambition, dreamed of the miracle of a poetic prose, musical yet without rhythm or rhyme, flexible enough and jarring enough to adapt to the lyrical movements of the soul, the undulations of reverie, the jolts of consciousness?" It's true, who among us hasn't dreamed of this? And it is not even a question of writing this poetic prose, but of feeling it, of finding this resonance.

Of course, you understand that this proposal is of no help when you can't sleep, that it is, on the contrary, an instruction manual for another awakening, for the *nuits debout*,[47] not the infinite awakening of 24/7 capitalism, but for its fierce, sovereign criticism. Because for the now, I can't sleep.

46. In addition to its historical, political, and philosophical perspectives, I find that one of the essential contributions of Achille Mbembe's thought is to link psychic life, political life, and economic life. Perhaps this is what Mbembe has most inherited from Frantz Fanon.

47. I am thinking here of "Nuit debout," the French and singularly Parisian version of the occupation movement that began in Madrid in 2011. "Occupy Paris," for obvious historical reasons, would have been in rather bad taste. So it was named "Nuit debout," which meant something else, namely a translation from space to time. This name also teaches us that these movements are, at their core, movements of awakening, aiming to put an end to the political and media hypnosis in which we are immersed. From the moment it was named, "Nuit debout" overdetermined its relationship to insomnia, to a temporal sequence that would not end any more than this interminable month of March, which went well beyond its thirty-one days.

"Nuit debout." An all-nighter, a night without rest, without sleep, an insomnia of several weeks, an interminable after-party that occupied less a square, in this case, Paris's Place de la République, than a time, in which we lived upright and awake, invigorated. And a night that would take possession of the calendar, creating a month of March that would never end, much like the never-ending month of March 2020[48] that inspired me to begin this text. In response to the occupation of days and nights by voracious capitalism, there was a critica and lucid counter-occupation of the night in the occupied squares of the whole world, with eyes wide open. And who cares if we die of exhaustion.

This occupation gave courage and pleasure, it even gave back pride, but it is not what would help me to sleep. I know it, I see it, I feel it, because it has exactly the consistency of my daytime reading, staccato. And it has the consistency of diaristic writing, which attracts me more and more, the consistency of the journal, in which one hears the word *jour*, the French "day," and never the word "night." It soothes me but does not put me to sleep.

That's right, I still can't sleep. So I turn to the crest of the windings and turnings of fancy: "I love the clouds—the clouds that pass—yonder—the marvellous clouds." I could indeed follow this lyrical movement as if it were a mantra, I could repeat it to myself ad infinitum, perhaps then I would fall asleep but I would not forget the preceding dialogue, its brutality, its brutal beauty, this awakening to language

48. "The Great Revolution introduced a new calendar. The initial day of a calendar presents history in time-lapse mode." Walter Benjamin, "On the Concept of History" [1940], in *Selected Writings, Volume 4, 1938–1940*, ed. Howard Eiland and Michael W. Jennings, trans. Edmund Jephcott, Howard Eiland, et al. (Cambridge, MA: Belknap Press of Harvard University Press, 2003), 395.

that the stranger convokes.[49] To convoke is a very big word, it assaults, and it hurts those of us who have believed or still sometimes believe in fathers, mothers, sisters, brothers, friends, in a country, in beauty, in gold, in everything that the foreigner who only loves "the clouds—the clouds that pass—yonder—the marvellous clouds" has broken with. Consciousness jolts.

The prince has not given up all this excitement, quite the contrary. He tells us that he is looking for poetic prose that is flexible enough and jarring enough to "adapt," the same words that voracious capitalism has set as masters in its neoliberal phase: adapt, jar, disrupt, but in a flexible, agile way.[50] He already perceives it, the collective soul of the future, the one that tortures me, he gives us the worm in the fruit of that bigger worm in the fruit. Before finding the clouds, one must cross through the "frequentation of

49. I give you the entire poem here, as an admirable convenience:

"Tell me, enigmatic man, whom do you love best? Your father, your mother, your sister, or your brother?

'I have neither father, nor mother, nor sister, nor brother.'

Your friends, then?

'You use a word that until now has had no meaning for me.'

Your country?

'I am ignorant of the latitude in which it is situated.'

Then Beauty?

'Her I would love willingly, goddess and immortal.'

Gold?

'I hate it as you hate your God.'

What, then, extraordinary stranger, do you love?

'I love the clouds—the clouds that pass—yonder—the marvellous clouds.'"

Charles Baudelaire, "The Stranger," in *The Poems and Prose Poems of Charles Baudelaire*, ed. James Huneker (1919), Project Gutenberg's public domain version, accessed August 15, 2020, https://www.gutenberg.org/files/36287/36287-h/36287-h.htm.

50. The incredible international resurgence of Victor Klemperer's *Language of the Third Reich: LTI, Lingua Tertii Imperii* (1957) shows us that his work on the Nazi language must be constantly taken up, continued, and deepened. In 2019, the first major trial was held in France against the managerial component of the neoliberal regime. Leaders of the formerly public, now privatized company France Telecom were prosecuted for a wave of suicides that struck a significant number of its management team. The president of the court, while pronouncing her verdict, which was rather harsh in her condemnation of the company's top commander, quoted a sentence from the notebooks of the philologist Klemperer: "Words can be like tiny doses of arsenic: you swallow them without noticing, they seem to have no effect, and after a while the toxic effect is felt."

huge cities" and through "the crossing of their innumerable relationships," whereas right now I want to go directly to the clouds. For the night, I don't need the cities and their relationships, this excess of lucidity, of course I would prefer a *nuit debout* to being awake 24/7, but still, when it comes to sleeping, I like the clouds even better.

That's why I abandon you, dear prince, at least at night, and I abandon myself to the clouds that I fantasize better than counting sheep, the same clouds perhaps as those that are seen by the bodies on my Facebook wall, the ones lying in the die-ins, wearing T-shirts that read "I can't breathe," because the clouds are better seen during the day and lying down than standing up at night. Here's what I'm thinking right now. That we need, as I read recently, a politics of napping,[51] that we need to listen carefully to what activist Tricia Hersey says and does with her Nap Ministry. That a nap could be a major political act that responds to the most important political question of our moment, that of the "universal right to breathe,"[52] because sleeping and breathing are almost synonymous.

I can('t) breathe = I can('t) sleep.

We've been believing in the clouds lately, when the world was on pause and you could actually see the clouds in the sky, without the planes and everything else. Very quickly, even "the city that never sleeps" plunged into sleep. The "frequentation of huge cities" and the "crossing of their innumerable relationships" gave way to emptiness, and when, in certain places, like the one where I live, one was finally allowed to go out, one did so as a flâneur and a dreamer.

51. Romain Bigé, "Nap-ins: Politiques de la sieste," *Pour un atlas des figures*, accessed September 24, 2020, https://www.pourunatlasdesfigures.net/element/nap-ins-politiques-de-la-sieste.

52. At least as formulated by Achille Mbembe; in French: "Le droit à la respiration universelle," *AOC*, April 6, 2020, https://aoc.media/opinion/2020/04/05/le-droit-universel-a-la-respiration/#__ftnref1. Or in a recent translation by Carolyn Shread, https://critinq.wordpress.com/2020/04/13/the-universal-right-to-breathe/.

But very quickly, also, when the world resumed its course, even when there were no planes in the sky, you could no longer see the clouds.

We only dreamed about one thing: stopping the world. "If we observe," writes Paul B., "the different shamanic rituals of Indigenous societies to 'stop the world,' we could say (drawing on the Brazilian anthropologist Eduardo Viveiros de Castro's analysis of Tupi rituals and shamanic practices) that they usually include at least three stages. In the first the subject is confronted with their mortality; in the second, they see their position in the trophic chain and perceive the energetic connections that unite all living things; in the final stage, they radically modify their desire, which will perhaps allow them to transform, to become someone else."[53] Luckily, some people have not forgotten, like I have, to make things explicit instead of drifting and connecting everything like the last of the romantics. And yet that too resonates, and it even resonates well, I can feel it, so I'm going to follow it a bit, because for me, sleep has long been part of what I imagine to be a shamanic ritual. Or at least a similar type of process. Isn't it a metamorphosis of daily life that awaits us when we become someone else, moving from wakefulness to sleep? Maybe we could even think of shamanic rituals as rituals that are intended to produce sleep, that were invented once sleep became a problem, because sleep has been a problem for a long time. And I even wonder if the renewed interest in shamanism is not proportional to capitalism's assault on sleep.

But when I say that, I also know very well how much uncertainty lies ahead. What do I know about shamans or shamanic rituals? Nothing more than what I'm reading here from a philosopher reading an anthropologist. Viveiros de Castro or Paul B. could say anything or understand nothing

53. Paul B. Preciado "On the Verge," *Artforum*, July/August 2020, accessed September 30, 2020, https://www.artforum.com/print/202006/paul-b-preciado-on-revolution-83286.

and I'd repeat it. So it's approximate. As my perception of my long association with post-exoticism is approximate.[54] It's a fact. But it's not so bad, because every time I hear that name, shamanism, I feel a vibration going down my spine, an animation, anima, maybe from what used to be called, because I don't think we call it that anymore, the reptilian brain. I see it as the ultimate reason or figure in the carpet of what I have, until now, devoted a good part of my life to. So I feel this animation every time I come across this name, shamanism. An animation coupled with a disappointment, because a shamanic ritual, I imagine, is something that is lived, not communicated. But all the same, if there is a moment when I feel like I am living an experience that brings me closer to it, it's when I can't sleep, and when my nocturnal readings work through my undulations, my sudden starts, my movements, anima. I feel then that something animates me that I do not possess and that does not possess me. So what Paul B. describes, after Viveiros de Castro, is what I don't always achieve and what I aspire to: a ritual to stop the world.

I imagine that the same thing has been repeated invariably over the thousands of years that the control of fire has allowed us to overcome the night, the cold, and so many dangers. I imagine that every time I turn on the light to resume reading this big book, it is because I'm resisting the world's standstill, that I am completely intoxicated by its rhythm, that I am unable to connect to the trophic chain and that I am clinging to a substitution chain, this fictional matrix supported by prosthetics, in this case, a book. I imagine that I fear the metamorphosis that sleep engenders in which I

54. To you, international reader: Since Paris is no longer the capital of the international republic of letters (cf. Pascale Casanova), you think there is nothing more to cut your teeth with than Michel Houellebecq or Leïla Slimani. But you should know that there are still great French works that sneak into being translated. In my opinion, the most contemporary of them all is Antoine Volodine's work, which comes under the name of post-exoticism. As far as English translations go, if you're curious, you'll be able to find an entire constellation of post-exotic authors and their fascinating works. For example, I recommend *Writers* (2010), in the translation by Katina Rogers, published by Dalkey Archive Press in 2014.

become, and only then, truly other. I imagine that at least I am conscious of this and that I prefer to be conscious of it, even if I fail often and deeply, where shamanic rituals probably succeed. But what do I have at my disposal, apart from the great fictional matrix borne by books and screens? Not much, I have to say. So it is to this chain of substitution that I entrust the task of yielding a passage, admittedly narrow, sometimes disappointing, towards the perception of the trophic chain. And even though I often suffer from it, I also cherish those moments of failure, when I turn the light back on, overcome by the sudden jolts of consciousness, and I tell myself that there is still hope, maybe next time, to stop the world, by following the undulations of reverie.

The Blue Hour

In the meantime, it's the blue hour, the end of the night.

And if by any chance someone wanted to know (and then I would want to know why they want to know) where I am at this hour, I would tell them to watch *Blue* by Apichatpong Weerasethakul.

I don't know about you, but I'm still a bit naive, I believe in the symbolic, in the image that says everything about a condition, that synthesizes it.[55] I know it's excessive, I know it's false, I know that it doesn't make any sense on the level of rationality, but then again, who's ever really been rational?

So last year, at the height of the fires that swept the world, and before the world got stuck, I thought that fire might be the symbol of our contemporary condition.[56]

55. "It's not that what is past casts its light on what is present, or what is present its light on the past; rather, image is that wherein what has been comes together in a flash with the now to form a constellation." Walter Benjamin, *Arcades Project*, 462 (Convolute N2a,3).

56. Notably in a cycle of conferences entitled "ABC des narrations" that I gave at the Maison de la Poésie in Paris. For more information, see https://www.maisondelapoesieparis.com/events/abc-des-narrations-1/.

Remember how it just didn't stop, fire was everywhere in our lives and in our dreams. And remember: California, Australia, Siberia, Notre Dame; the fires at the "gilet jaune' demonstrations in France or the pro-democracy protests in Hong Kong; remember the finale of *Game of Thrones* and th images from the series *Chernobyl*; remember how mainstrea culture was fascinated by fire, remember the Grammy Awar stage, where Tyler, The Creator presented a metaphor for the era, in which the only thing to do is to shoot oneself in th head before throwing oneself into the blaze.[57]

Yes, the world and our dreams seemed to be on fire, that's what I ended up thinking.

It was thus that walls of flame presented themselves to me, and, oh, how they seemed impassable, but the blue hour had finally come, and I knew that it was not with the flames that I would be able to sleep. Soon, these flames will turn int a torrent of repetitive images that no longer communicate, they loop around and lead to nothing. I know in my heart that I have to leave the main stream, the mainstream where these same obsessive images repeat themselves, *gnangnangnangna* always the same loop, always at full speed, always without a solution. I know that we have to be able to travel in the run-offs, in the fragile streams where life can be reborn. It doesn' matter which ones, as long as they are modest, gentle, and minor.

So, to finish, I come out of the torrent of repetitive images that imposed itself on me, from *Game of Thrones* to *Chernobyl* to Tyler, The Creator. They fascinate me, but the bewilder me, alienate me, and keep me awake, so I take the runoff, the *Blue* of Apichatpong Weerasethakul, which will join soon, the *Cemetery of Splendour*, then *Uncle Boonmee*.[58]

Yes, in order to find sleep, it is in this direction (against

57. Watch Tyler, The Creator's performance at the 2020 Grammy Awards here: https://www.youtube.com/watch?v=IJilkMPqvs0.

58. Three films by Apichatpong Weerasethakul: *Uncle Boonmee Who Can Recall His Past Lives* (2010); *Cemetery of Splendour* (2015); *Blue* (2018).

chronology) that I must go, and that I will go again. So I start with the last one, *Blue*, the shortest, the most artsy, the most symbolic, because of the three films it performs the best synthesis. I recognize myself in the woman, played by Weerasethakul's favorite actress, Jenjira Pongpas. Like me, she twist and turns in her bed, under a thick blanket. She lies on her back, her hands folded, in a prayer, while a painted panel rolls up to show another panel unfolding. And despite the overwhelming noise of the surrounding jungle, we can hear footsteps approaching, the click of a lighter, and the flame takes over the woman's body. It takes and it grows, it consumes a part of the painted scenery, and probably of the jungle. Her insomnia turns into fire. Everything is linked, fire, sleep, narration, cinema, life or death.

The woman stays calm, the movie stays calm. And her calmness calms me.

Because I can see the superimposition of the two images that I have to undo. I think, again, that one can always cut the lighted fuse, before the spark reaches the dynamite.[59] I also think of this when I see *Cemetery of Splendour*, that cradle of splendor, in which, unlike in *Blue*, soldiers are struck by a mysterious sleeping sickness that plunges them into a deep lethargy. We understand, or we understand as best as we can, because nothing is really very explicit, and thank you, Joe (because that's your nickname), for that, for not being quite explicit, it does us good, yes, we understand all the same, when two goddesses appear as very modern young women that the modern people have modified the trophic chain of the world by building, on top of an old palace, a school, and then a dispensary, and who knows what else to come, under the force of the shovels, on a new building site. And then they forgot. The ones before us also modified it,

59. "Before the spark reaches the dynamite, the lighted fuse must be cut." Walter Benjamin, *One-Way Street* [1928], trans. Edmund Jephcott (Cambridge, MA: Belknap Press of Harvard University Press, 2016).

with their palace built on top of a cemetery. And they also forgot. Then the spirit of a king haunts the soldiers who can do nothing but sleep.

I go up the chain again and I finally get to Uncle Boonmee, who remembers his past lives. Unlike what the moderns have done to the ancient palace, itself built on a cemetery, he revisits and he remembers.

So he can die, and I can sleep.

LETTER FROM CHARLES BAUDELAIRE TO ARSÈNE HOUSSAYE

Translated by Claire Finch

My dear friend,

I'm sending you a little book that, without injustice, could be said to have neither head nor tail, since everything, on the contrary, is both head and tail, alternately and reciprocally. Consider, would you, what admirable convenience this combination offers to all of us: to you, to me, and to the reader. We can cut wherever we want, I can cut my reverie, you the manuscript, the reader his reading; because I do not suspend the reader's restive will from the endless thread of a fine-spun plot.[60] Take out a vertebra, and the two pieces of this tortuous fantasy will rejoin, easily. Chop it into many fragments, and you will see that each can exist on its own. In the hope that some of these chunks will be alive enough to please and

60. Translator's note: I tripped over the multiple masculine universals in this letter, the reader with "his" reading, the poet with "his" craft. I had initially translated both of these instances using the gender-inclusive "their." This would have been the Anglophone equivalent of the gender-inclusive pronouns that French writers are fighting to use in official writing, such as *iel* (instead of *il* or *elle*) or *celleux* (instead of *ceux* or *celles*). But to do so would have erased something that is part of Baudelaire's writing, and that is still present when we use him to talk about contemporaneity: how his modernist inventions, which are advanced through his romanticization of "minor" figures and lives, depend on an exoticization (in the case of Jeanne Duval) or else a disgusted fascination (in the case of women in general, and older women in particular). So when you're translating Baudelaire as a queer and feminist person you have to keep these problems in there, perhaps as another "alert," to borrow from Lionel Ruffel's text. See Lisa Robertson's excellent poetic reclaiming of Baudelaire for feminine and AFAB people, in "Proverbs of a She-Dandy," *Buenos Tiempos, Int.* (2017); and *The Baudelaire Fractal* (Toronto: Coach House Books, 2020).

amuse you, I dare to dedicate the entire snake to you.

I have a little confession to make. It was while flipping for the twentieth time at least through Aloysius Bertrand's famous *Gaspard de la nuit* (a book that's known to you, to me, and to some of our friends, so doesn't it have every right to be called famous?) that the idea came to me to try something similar, and to apply to the description of modern life, or rather to a single and more abstract modern life, the same process that he used to depict ancient life, so strangely picturesque.

Which of us has not, in his days of ambition, dreamed of the miracle of a poetic prose, musical yet without rhythm or rhyme, flexible enough and jarring enough to adapt to the lyrical movements of the soul, the undulations of reverie,[61] the jolts of consciousness?

It is especially the frequentation of huge cities, the crossing of their innumerable relationships, that gives birth to this obsessive ideal. Haven't you, my dear friend, ever tried to translate the window fitter's strident cry into a song, or tried to express in lyrical prose every desolate suggestion that this cry sends all the way to the attic rooms, through the street's highest mists?

But, to tell you the truth, I'm afraid that my jealousy has not brought me good luck. As soon as I started working, I realized not only that I was still very far from my mysterious and brilliant model, but also that I was doing something (if this thing can be called something) singularly different, an accident of which anyone besides me might be proud, but which can only deeply humiliate a mind that regards it as the poet's greatest honor to achieve exactly what he had planned to do.

Devotedly yours,

C. B.

61. Another choice might have been "daydream." But we chose "reverie" here, in order to echo the English translation of Rousseau's *Reveries of the Solitary Walker* (1782).

BIBLIOGRAPHY

Les associés d'EIM. *Les dirigeants français et le changement.* Paris: Éditions Huitème Jour, 2004.

Avanessian, Armen, and Suhail Malik, eds. *Time Complex: Post-contemporary.* Miami, FL: [NAME], 2016.

Barthes, Roland. *The Preparation of the Novel: Lecture Courses and Seminars at the Collège de France (1978–1979 and 1979–1980).* New York: Columbia University Press, 2010.

Baschet, Jérôme. *Adieux au capitalism: Autonomie, société du bien vivre et multiplicité des mondes.* Paris: La Découverte, 2016.

Bataille, Georges. *La notion de dépense.* 1933; Paris: Lignes, 2011.

Baudelaire, Charles. "Correspondances." In *Les fleurs du mal.* Paris: Auguste Poulet-Malassis, 1857.

——. "L'étranger." In *Le spleen de Paris* [1869]. Accessed September 30, 2020. https://fr.wikisource.org/wiki/L'Étranger.

——. "Lettre à Arsène Houssaye." December 20, 1861. Accessed September 30, 2020. https://fr.wikisource.org/wiki/À–Arsène–Houssaye–(Baudelaire).

——. "The Old Mountebank." Translated by Joseph T. Shipley. In *Baudelaire: His Prose and Poetry*, edited by T. R. Smith. Accessed August 12, 2020. https://www.gutenberg.org/files/47032/47032-h/47032-h.htm#Page–66.

——. "Le vieux saltimbanque." In *Le spleen de Paris* [1869]. Accessed September 30, 2020. https://fr.wikisource.org/wiki/Le__Vieux__Saltimbanque.

Benjamin, Walter. "Convolute N: On the Theory of Knowledge, Theory of Progress." In *The Arcades Project*, translated by Howard Eiland and Kevin McLaughlin, 456–488. Cambridge, MA: Belknap Press of Harvard University Press, 1999.

——. "On the Concept of History" [1940]. In *Selected Writings, Volume 4, 1938–1940*, edited by Howard Eiland and Michael W. Jennings, translated by Edmund Jephcott, Howard Eiland, et al. Cambridge, MA: Belknap Press of Harvard University Press, 2003.

——. *One-Way Street* [1928]. Translated by Edmund Jephcott. Cambridge, MA: Belknap Press of Harvard University Press, 2016.

——. "The Storyteller: Observations on the Works of Nikolai Leskov" [1936]. In *Selected Writings, Volume 3, 1935–1938*, edited by Howard Eiland and Michael W. Jennings, translated by Edmund Jephcott, Howard Eiland, et al., 143–166. Cambridge, MA: Belknap Press of Harvard University Press, 2002.

Bigé, Romain. "Nap-ins: Politiques de la sieste." *Pour un atlas des figures*. Accessed September 24, 2020. https://www.pourunatlasdesfigures.net/element/nap-ins-politiques-de-la-sieste.

Bolaño, Roberto. *The Savage Detectives* [1998]. Translated by Natasha Wimmer. New York: Farrar, Straus & Giroux, 2007.

Boullier, Dominique. "Les industries de l'attention: Fidélisation, alerte ou immersion." *Réseaux*, no. 154 (2009/2): 231–246.

Casanova, Pascale. *Kafka, Angry Poet* [2011]. Translated by Chris Turner. Kolkata: Seagull Books, 2015.
——. "The Literary Greenwich Meridian: Some Thoughts on the Temporal Forms of Literary Belief." In *Field Day Review*, no. 4 (2008): 7–23.
——. *The World Republic of Letters* [1999]. Translated by Malcolm DeBevoise. Cambridge, MA: Harvard University Press, 2005.

Citton, Yves. *Mythocratie: Storytelling et imaginaire de gauche*. Paris: La Découverte, 2010.

Crary, Jonathan. *Suspensions of Perception: Attention, Spectacle, and Modern Culture*. Cambridge, MA: MIT Press, 2000.
——. *24/7: Late Capitalism and the Ends of Sleep*. London: Verso, 2013.

Deleuze, Giles. *Différence et répétition*. Paris: Presses Universitaires de France, 1968.

Deleuze, Gilles, and Félix Guattari. *L'anti-Œdipe: Capitalisme et schizophrénie 1*. Paris: Éditions de Minuit, 1972.
——. *Kafka, pour une littérature mineure*. Paris: Éditions de Minuit, 1975.
——. *Mille plateaux: Capitalisme et schizophrénie 2*. Paris: Éditions de Minuit, 1980.
——. *Qu'est-ce que la philosophie?* Paris: Éditions de Minuit, 1991.

Denk, Felix, and Sven von Thülen. *Der Klang der Familie: Berlin, Techno and the Fall of the Wall*. Norderstedt: Books on Demand, 2014.

Descola, Philippe. *La composition des mondes: Entretiens avec Pierre Charbonnier*. Paris: Flammarion, 2014.

Despret, Vinciane. *Au bonheur des morts: Récits de ceux qui restent*. Paris: La Découverte, 2015.

Fuller, Matthew. *How to Sleep: The Art, Biology and Culture of Unconsciousness.* London: Bloomsbury, 2018.

Garcia, Tristan. *The Life Intense: A Modern Obsession.* Translated by Abigail RayAlexander, Christopher RayAlexander, and Jon Cogburn. Edinburgh: Edinburgh University Press, 2018.

Huet, Romain. *Le vertige de l'émeute: De la Zad aux Gilets jaunes.* Paris: Presses Universitaires de France, 2019.

Kafka, Franz. *Diaries, 1910–1923.* Translated by Joseph Kresh and Martin Greenberg. New York: Schocken, 2009.

Klemperer, Victor. *Language of the Third Reich: LTI, Lingua Tertii Imperil* [1957]. London: Bloomsbury, 2013.

Lefebvre, Noémi. *Poétique de l'emploi.* Paris: Verticales, 2018.

Mbembe, Achille. *Brutalisme.* Paris: La Découverte, 2020.
——. "Le droit à la respiration universelle." *AOC*, April 6, 2020. https://aoc.media/opinion. /2020/04/05/le-droit-universel-a-la-respiration/#__ftnref1.
——. "The Universal Right to Breathe." Translated by Carolyn Shread. *Critical Inquiry Blog*, April 13, 2020. https://critinq .wordpress.com/2020/04/13/the-universal-right-to-breathe/.

Nerval, Gérard de. "Le Christ aux oliviers." In *Les chimères*, 295–297. Paris: Michel Lévy Frères, 1856.

Pachet, Pierre. *La force de dormir.* Paris: Gallimard, 1988.

Preciado, Paul B. "On the Verge." *Artforum*, July/August 2020. Accessed September 30, 2020. https://www.artforum.com /print/202006/paul-b-preciado-on-revolution-83286.

Quintane, Nathalie. *Les années 10.* Paris: Fabrique, 2014.

Robertson, Lisa. *The Baudelaire Fractal.* Toronto: Coach House Books, 2020.
——. "Proverbs of a She-Dandy." *Buenos Tiempos, Int.*, 2017. http://buenostiemposinternational.com/files/Lisa-Robertson __Proverbs-of-a-She-Dandy__Buenos-Tiempos-Int__2017.pdf.

Ruffel, Lionel. *Brouhaha: Worlds of the Contemporary* [2016]. Translated by Raymond McKenzie. Minneapolis: University of Minnesota Press, 2018.
——. *Trompe-la-mort.* Paris: Verdier, 2019.

Salmon, Christian. *Storytelling: Bewitching the Modern Mind* [2008]. Translated by David Macey. London: Verso, 2010.

Samoyault, Tiphaine. *Traduction et violence*. Paris: Éditions du Seuil, 2020.

Schaeffer, Jean-Marie. *Why Fiction?* [1999]. Translated by Dorrit Cohn. Lincoln: Nebraska University Press, 2010.

Scott, James C. *Against the Grain: A Deep History of the Earliest State*. New Haven, CT: Yale University Press, 2018.

Shakespeare, William. *Tragédies I: Œuvres complètes I. Édition bilingue*. Edited by Jean Michel Desprats. Paris: Gallimard, 2002.

Simon, Claude. *Les Géorgiques*. Paris: Éditions de Minuit, 1981.
——. *Histoire*. Paris: Éditions de Minuit, 1967.
——. *Le jardin des plantes*. Paris: Éditions de Minuit, 1997.
——. *The Trolley* [2001]. Translated by Richard Howard. New York: New Press, 2004.

Sontag, Susan. *Illness as Metaphor and AIDS and Its Metaphors*. London: Picador, 2001.

Stiegler, Bernard. *What Makes Life Worth Living: On Pharmacology* [2010]. Translated by Daniel Ross. Cambridge: Polity, 2013.

Szendy, Peter. *Hits: Philosophy in the Jukebox* [2008]. Translated by Will Bishop. New York: Fordham University Press, 2012.

Vila-Matas, Enrique. *A Brief History of Portable Literature* [1985]. Translated by Anne McLean and Thomas Bunstead. New York: New Directions, 2015.

Volodine, Antoine. *Writers* [2010]. Translated by Katina Rogers. Chicago: Dalkey Archive Press, 2014.

FILMS AND PERFORMANCES

L'abécédaire de Gilles Deleuze. Produced by Pierre-André Boutang, 1988–89. Aired 1995 on Arte. YouTube playlist, accessed September 30, 2020. https://www.youtube.com/playlist?list=PLiR8NqajHNPbaX2rBoA2z6IPGpU0IPIS2.

Baumbach, Noah, dir. *Marriage Story*. Los Gatos, CA: Netflix, 2019.

Devs. Season 1. Directed by Alex Garland. Aired March 5–April 16, 2020 on Hulu.

Truffaut, François, dir. *Domicile conjugal*. Los Angeles, CA: Columbia, 1970.

Tyler, The Creator. "Tyler, The Creator – EARFQUAKE / NEW MAGIC WAND (Live at the 2020 GRAMMYs)." YouTube video, 4:43, January 29, 2020. https://www.youtube.com/watch?v=lJilkMPqvs0.

Wachowskis, dir. *The Matrix*. Burbank, CA: Warner Bros., 1999.
——. *The Matrix Reloaded*. Burbank, CA: Warner Bros., 2003.
——. *The Matrix Revolutions*. Burbank, CA: Warner Bros., 2003.

Weerasethakul, Apichatpong, dir. *Uncle Boonmee Who Can Recall His Past Lives*. Bangkok: Kick the Machine Films, 2010.
——. *Cemetery of Splendour*. Bangkok: Kick the Machine Films, 2015.
——. *Blue*. Paris: OnP/Les Films Pelléas, 2018. https://www.operadeparis.fr/3e-scene/blue.

Westworld. Season 3. "The New World." Aired March 15–May 3, 2020 on HBO.

Lionel Ruffel is a literary scholar, publisher, and author. Chair and Professor of Comparative Literature at University of Paris 8, he is the founding director of the creative writing program there. From 2011 to 2016, he held the Research Chair in Archaeology of the Contemporary (Literatures, Cultures, Knowledges) at the French University Institute. Among his recent projects, he has organized (together with artist Kader Attia) "Theory Now" at La Colonie (Paris), "The Publishing Sphere" at the Haus der Kulturen der Welt (Berlin), and "Radio Brouhaha" at Centre Pompidou (Paris). Ruffel is also the author of four monographs: *Le dénouement* (2005); *Volodine post-exotique* (2007); *Brouhaha: Worlds of the Contemporary* (2016 in French, 2018 in English), *Trompe-la-mort* (2019), and over forty book chapters and articles, published in five languages.

Claire Finch is a writer, performer, and researcher based in Paris whose work focuses on queer poetic protocols and their links with feminist activism. She tours widely, giving performative readings and conferences on objects such as the textual dildo or vomit as an emancipatory literary form. Recent publications include *Kathy Acker 1971–1975* (2019), and her French translation of Lisa Robertson's *Debbie: An Epic* (with sabrina soyer, 2021).

PEN=0,3,1,20, WEIGHT=120, SLANT=0, SUPERNESS=0.5

The typeface used to set this series is called Meta-the-difference-between-the-two-Font (MTDBT2F), designed by Dexter Sinister in 2010 after MetaFont, a digital typography system originally programmed by computer scientist Donald Kunth in 1979.

Unlike more common digital outline fonts formats such as TrueType o Postscript, a MetaFont is constructed of strokes drawn with set-widt pens. Instead of describing each of the individual shapes that make up a family of related characters, a MetaFont file describes only the basic pen path or *skeleton* letter. Perhaps better imagined as the ghost that comes in advance of a particular letterform, a MetaFont character is defined only by a set of equations. It is then possible to tweak various parameters such as weight, slant, and superness (more or less bold, italic, and a form of chutzpah) in order to generate endless variations on the same bare bones.

Meta-the-difference-between-the-two-Font is essentially the same as MetaFont, abiding the obvious fact that it swallows its predecessor. Although the result may look the same, it clearly can't be, because in addition to the software, the new version embeds its own backstory. In this sense, MTDBT2F is not only a tool to generate countless PostScript fonts, but *at least equally* a tool to think about and around MetaFont. Mathematician Douglas Hofstadter once noted that one of the best things MetaFont might do is inspire readers to chase after the intelligence of an alphabet, and "yield new insights into the elusive "spirits" that flit about so tantalizingly behind those lovely shapes we call "letters.""

For instance, each volume in The Contemporary Condition is set in a new MTDBT2F, generated at the time of publication, which is to say *now.*

Dexter Sinister, 22/06/21, 17:04 PM